EVOLUTION

Charlotte Luongo

This edition first published in 2010 in the United States
of America by Marshall Cavendish Benchmark.

Marshall Cavendish Benchmark
99 White Plains Road
Tarrytown, NY 10591
www.marshallcavendish.us

All Internet addresses were available and accurate when this book went to press.

Library of Congress Cataloging-in-Publication Data
Luongo, Charlotte.
Evolution / by Charlotte Luongo.
p. cm.—(Big ideas in science)
Summary: "Provides comprehensive information on evolution
and how it affects our lives today"—Provided by publisher.
Includes bibliographical references and index.
ISBN 978-0-7614-4393-3
1. Evolution (Biology)—Juvenile literature.
2. Darwin, Charles, 1809–1882—Juvenile literature.
3. Natural selection—Juvenile literature. I. Title.
QH367.1.L86 2010
576.8—dc22
2009002557

The photographs in this book are used by permission and through the courtesy of:
Cover: Yan Ke/Shutterstock; Q2AMedia Art Bank
Half Title: Elizabeth Netterstrom/Alamy
pp4-5: De Agostini Picture Library/Getty Images; p5 (inset): James Steidl/Fotolia; p6: Photolibrary;
p7: The Gallery Collection/Corbis; p8: Bettmann/Corbis; p9: Michael Nicholson/Corbis;
p10: Michael Zysman; p12: Elizabeth Netterstrom/Alamy; p15: Jim Mills/Shutterstock;
p16tr: James Davis/Eye Ubiquitous/Corbis; p16bl: Photolibrary; pp18-19: Dreamstime;
pp20-21: Istockphoto; pp22-23: 123RF; p23 (inset): Dreamstime; p26: Mary Evan Picture Library/Photolibrary;
p27: Hulton-Deutsch Collection/Corbis; p29: NASA; p31: Frans Lanting/Corbis; p34: Istockphoto;
p35: Dreamstime; p36: National Library of Medicine; p39: Tose/Dreamstime; p41: Science Photo Library;
pp42-43: Corey C. Fake, copyright 2006 (July); p42 (inset): Istockphoto; p44: Photolibrary.
Illustrations: Q2AMedia Art Bank

Created by Q2AMedia
Art Director: Sumit Charles
Editor: Denise Pangia
Series Editor: Penny Dowdy
Client Service Manager: Santosh Vasudevan
Project Manager: Shekhar Kapur
Designer: Shilpi Sarkar and Prashant Kumar
Illustrators: Prachand Verma, Ajay Sharma,
Bibin Jose, Abhideep Jha and Rajesh Das
Photo Research: Shreya Sharma

Printed in Malaysia

1 3 5 6 4 2

Contents

Introduction

Imagine you are transported back in time. You are still in North America, but you are 50 million years in the past. You find yourself in a swamp. You see some familiar-looking plants. You even see a few spiders. Then, suddenly you hear footsteps coming toward you. Out of the leaves dashes a huge beast! It has a giant head and sharp claws. It stands over 7 feet (2 meters) tall—taller than most adult humans. Its two legs are long and powerful.

What on earth could this creature be? Is it a dinosaur? Could it be a mammoth? In fact, it is neither one. This strange creature is the cousin of a very common animal. What you are seeing is a distant relative of the chicken.

This ancient animal is called a *Diatryma*. Fossils of this bird are found across the United States. Over many millions of years, giant birds like the Diatryma changed. They became smaller. Their jaws became less powerful. They started to look like the birds that you see today.

Diatryma

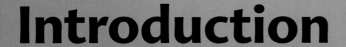

What caused this change? How could the giant Diatryma be related to modern birds? The answers to both of these questions can be found in a very important scientific **theory**: the theory of evolution. This theory provides the foundation on which all the life sciences are based.

The Diatryma is a distant relative of the chicken.

Charles Darwin
A Man with Many Questions

The Galápagos Islands are home to many animals. There are turtles, lizards, sea lions, and birds. One type of bird is the finch, which is a small songbird. There are thirteen different kinds of finches on the Galápagos Islands.

All of the finches on the Galápagos Islands are closely related. So how did they become so different from one another? Many of them don't look much like finches at all. Some of them live on the ground. Some of them live in trees. Some have short, round beaks. Others have thin beaks like tweezers. One type of finch is black. Another type has olive-colored feathers. You may also find gray and brown finches.

In addition to looking different, the Galápagos finches eat different things. Some kinds of finches eat insects. Others eat berries. There is also a kind of finch that attacks other birds. This finch is known as a vampire finch. It jumps on the backs of larger birds. It pecks at the birds until they begin to bleed, and then it feeds on their blood.

There are many different kinds of finches on the Galápagos Islands. This finch lives on the ground. It has a strong beak that it uses to break seeds and nuts.

Why does one kind of finch live in trees and another kind make nests on the ground? Why do the finches have such different beaks? These were questions that Charles Darwin asked. Darwin was a man fascinated by nature.

Charles Darwin was born in England on February 12, 1809. As a child, Darwin collected minerals and insects. He also enjoyed bird-watching. In college, Darwin took some classes about plants and animals. Yet, he did not think he would make a career out of it. All that changed in August 1831.

Charles Darwin's father and grandfather were both doctors. Medicine was the family business. Darwin's oldest brother also became a doctor. When Darwin set off for college, his family expected him to be a doctor, too. But, Darwin had no interest in medicine. He decided to join the clergy instead. He went to Cambridge University to study to be a preacher. Darwin did well in all of his classes, but his heart was not in it. He took science classes on the side. Before long, he had impressed many of his science teachers. They convinced him to pursue a new career.

From a young age, Charles Darwin loved studying nature. He was interested in all living things, including insects, birds, plants, and fish.

Ideas That Shaped Darwin's Thinking

Darwin finished his studies in 1831. A few months later he received an interesting letter that changed his life. Darwin was invited on a trip to sail around the world.

The ship was called the HMS *Beagle*. Its mission was to map the coast of South America. The captain of the ship also wanted to collect scientific data along the way. The captain decided to invite a scientist to come with him. One of Darwin's science teachers suggested that Darwin would be a good choice. Darwin was thrilled when he got the letter. It seemed like the chance of a lifetime. Not only would he get to see the world, he would also be able to pursue his interest in studying nature.

Darwin immediately began to prepare for the voyage. He packed many science books to read on the trip. After reading these books and others, Darwin had an idea that would change the entire science of **biology**, which is the study of organisms, or living things.

Darwin only had a few weeks to prepare for his trip on the *Beagle*. Before he left, he talked with many scientists about how to preserve the plant and animal specimens he planned to collect.

Some of the books Darwin read were written by French scientist Jean-Baptiste Lamarck. Lamarck had studied many different fossils, which are remains or impressions in the earth of ancient living things. Fossils show what living things were like in the past. It seemed clear to Lamarck that fossilized organisms were different than organisms that are still in existence. From this observation, Lamarck decided that living things had changed over time.

Jean-Baptiste Lamarck was born into a military family. As expected, he became a soldier himself, but he was injured and forced to leave the army. This was when he became interested in science.

When Lamarck began studying biology, most other scientists ignored invertebrates, or animals without bones (for example, insects and worms). Most people in the late 1700s thought invertebrates were very simple and not very important. Lamarck disagreed. He spent a great deal of time learning about them. In fact, it was Lamarck who first came up with the word *invertebrate*. The modern classification system for invertebrates is based on Lamarck's work.

Lamarck was certain that living things could change, but he was not sure how. He suggested that perhaps a living thing could change during its lifetime in order to **adapt**, or adjust, to a particular **environment**.

Lamarck used a water bird as an example. He thought that the bird's legs would begin to grow longer if it were always wading in deep water looking for food. The legs would lengthen only a little over the bird's lifetime, but this change would then be passed on to its offspring, or children. The offsprings' legs might also grow, and that increase in length would be passed to the next group of offspring, or the next **generation**. So, each new generation of water birds would have slightly longer legs.

Today we know that Lamarck's ideas are not correct. But, Darwin was convinced that Lamarck was right about one thing: living things do change over time.

Jean-Baptiste Lamarck thought that the legs of a water bird, such as a flamingo, would grow longer if the bird were always fishing in deep water.

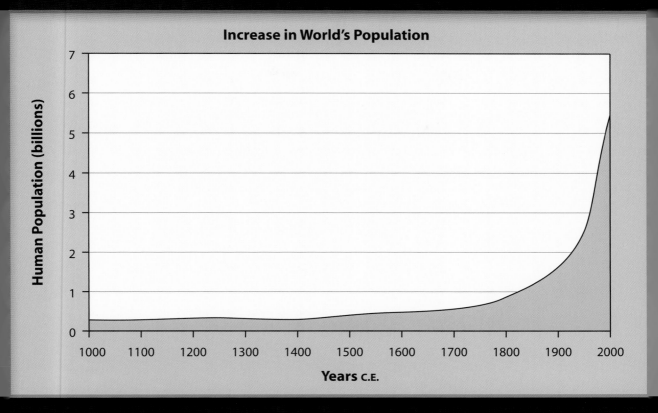

Increase in World's Population

Thomas Malthus saw that the human population was growing at a fast rate, but realized that this growth could not continue forever.

Darwin also read a scientific paper written by Thomas Malthus. Malthus was interested in how populations grow. A population is a group of living things residing in the same place. For example, all of the people in a city make up the city's population. Malthus saw that many populations in Europe were growing quickly. The cities were becoming overcrowded. Malthus thought that if the population kept growing this way, there would not be enough food for everybody. There would also not be enough living space.

Thomas Malthus lived from 1766 to 1834. During his life, the population of the United Kingdom nearly doubled. Part of the reason for this was improved medical care for children. When Malthus was born, about seven out of every ten children born in London died before they grew up. By the end of Malthus's life, only three out of ten children died. This caused the population to grow. As a result, London became very crowded and very polluted. Malthus saw many poor and hungry people. He blamed all of these problems on the uncontrolled growth of the population.

Malthus realized that a population could not grow forever. Eventually, there would be something that would limit its size. For example, a population could run out of food. When this happened, many people would starve. This would keep the population from becoming too large.

Darwin saw that Malthus's ideas were true for all living things, not just people. For example, one insect can lay millions of eggs every year. Suppose all of these eggs hatched. All of the young insects would then lay millions of eggs themselves. These eggs would hatch, too. Soon, the world would be overrun by insects. Darwin concluded from this that not all offspring in a species survive. Those that did survive were probably the healthiest and strongest.

This monarch butterfly is laying an egg. A single butterfly can lay about 700 eggs in a year. If all the eggs hatch and each new butterfly lays 700 eggs, there would be a total of 490,000 eggs. If all of these eggs hatched and the offspring laid their own eggs, there would be 343 million eggs.

This "survival of the fittest" idea was very important. It would help Darwin understand how living things could change over time.

How much time does it take for organisms to change? Part of the answer to this question came from yet another book. A year before Darwin sailed on the HMS *Beagle*, the book *Principles of Geology* was published. It was written by Charles Lyell, who argued three points. First, most of Earth's features were made by very slow processes. Second, the processes that changed Earth in the past are still happening today. Third, in order for Earth's features to form slowly, Earth must be very old. Lyell thought Earth must be millions or even billions of years old.

While on his trip, Darwin witnessed an earthquake. It caused a rocky shore to rise 10 feet (3 m) out of the sea. When Darwin saw this, he realized Lyell must be right. Very slowly over time, thousands of such earthquakes could form a mountain range. So, Earth must be very old. This allowed plenty of time for organisms to change.

Charles Lyell strongly disagreed with Jean-Baptiste Lamarck and wrote many papers criticizing his ideas. In one paper, Lyell used the example of a giraffe's neck to make fun of Lamarck's ideas about how living things change. If Lamarck were right, wrote Lyell, a giraffe's neck would keep stretching over its lifetime because it had to reach high for its food. Today, many textbooks incorrectly use the example of the giraffe's neck to explain Lamarck's ideas. Yet, the example actually came from Lyell, who was using it to mock Lamarck!

1831
Charles Darwin sets sail on the HMS *Beagle*. He will travel around the world.

1830
Charles Lyell publishes *Principles of Geology*. Lyell proposes that the same processes that changed Earth in the past are still at work today.

1809
Jean-Baptiste Lamarck describes how he thinks organisms change over time.

1798
Thomas Malthus predicts that the human population cannot continue to grow forever. War or a lack of food or space would eventually stop the population's growth.

The Voyage of the *Beagle*

When the HMS *Beagle* set sail in 1831, its mission was to map the coast of South America. The government did not send the ship to make scientific discoveries. However, information learned on the *Beagle's* trip would change science forever.

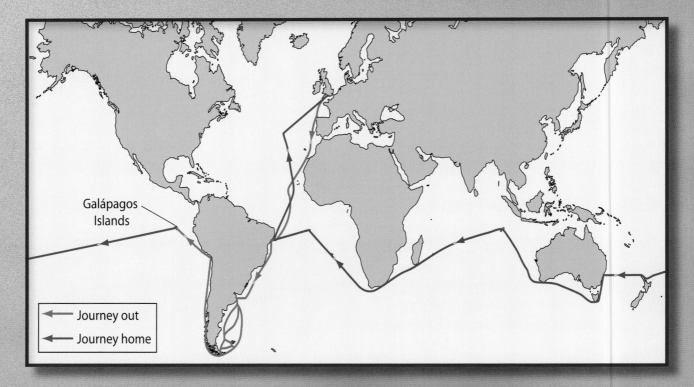

Galápagos Islands

← Journey out
← Journey home

The HMS *Beagle* traveled to several continents and stopped at many islands. At each stop, Charles Darwin recorded what he observed. He drew pictures of the different organisms he saw. He wrote notes describing the behavior of the animals: what they ate, how they acted, and where they lived.

The HMS *Beagle* took five years to sail around the world.

Darwin also collected many specimens, or samples, of different plants and animals. On one walk through a forest in Brazil, Darwin collected specimens of sixty-eight different kinds of beetles!

On the trip, Darwin began to notice similar environments all over the world. For example, there were grasslands in Africa, Australia, and South America. In addition, animals with similar characteristics lived in those grasslands. Ostriches, which are large birds that do not fly, could be found in the African grasslands. Rheas, which look a lot like ostriches and also do not fly, lived in the American grasslands. The emu, another large, flightless bird, lived in the Australian grasslands.

Darwin began to wonder about all of this. Why did all of these large, flightless birds live in grasslands and not in forests? Darwin also wondered why the flightless birds in the South American grasslands, for example, weren't exactly the same as those in Africa. These observations and questions led Darwin to an important conclusion: living things around the world develop differently. Yet, living things in similar environments develop many similar characteristics.

Ostriches live in Africa. Yet they are similar to rheas and emus, which live on different continents.

Charles Darwin was only twenty-two years old when he left England on the HMS *Beagle.* The ship was very small. It measured only 90 feet (27 m) long. That's less than one-third of a football field. There were seventy-four men on the ship. There was very little space. Many men in the crew did not think the *Beagle* was a good ship for crossing the ocean. Its small size meant it was easy for large waves to rock the ship from side to side. This turned out to be a problem for Darwin. He was seasick most of the time. Darwin got off the boat and went ashore every chance he got.

15

Darwin also saw that organisms could vary locally. For example, he saw that not all rheas were the same. Some rheas lived in warm grasslands. Other rheas lived in cold, dry grasslands. The two groups of rheas were different. The rheas that lived in the cold grasslands were smaller. They also had thicker feathers.

Next, Darwin traveled to the Galápagos Islands, which are in the Pacific Ocean off the coast of Ecuador. There, Darwin had dinner with the governor of the islands, and tortoise meat was served. A tortoise is similar to a turtle. The governor told Darwin that he could tell which island the tortoise came from by looking at its shell. This surprised Darwin. Why didn't the same kind of tortoise live on all the islands of the Galápagos? Why were the tortoises on each island slightly different?

Darwin began looking closely at the tortoises. He saw that tortoises on Isabella Island had dome-shaped shells and short necks. The tortoises on Hood Island were not like this. They had long necks, and their shells were open around the neck.

Tortoises on Isabella Island have short necks and dome-shaped shells. They mostly eat plants that are close to the ground.

Tortoises on Hood Island have long necks and open shells. This helps them reach leaves on tall plants.

Location of the Galápagos Islands

N

Location of Galápagos Islands

Pinta (Abingdon)

Genovesa (Tower)

Marchena (Bindloe)

Santiago (James)   Bartolome

Sombrero Clino

Rabida (Jervis)   Daphne   Baltra   Seymour Norte

Fernandina (Narborough)

San Cristobal (Chatham)

Pinzon (Duncan)   Santa Cruz

Isabella

Santa Fe (Barrinton)

Tortuga   Floreana (Charles)

Espanola (Hood)

Charles Darwin spent five weeks on the Galápagos Islands. There, he studied the differences between the organisms on the various islands.

Darwin thought these differences could be explained by the environment. On Isabella Island there were many plants. These plants were low to the ground, so it was easy for tortoises with short necks to get food. Hood Island was different. It had fewer plants, and most of those plants were very tall. So, only a tortoise with a long neck could survive there.

Studying rheas and tortoises helped Darwin see that organisms are well suited to their environments. He recognized that organisms have adaptations, or changes that develop to help them survive in specific conditions.

Darwin collected a huge number of specimens on his trip. On a stop at one island, he hiked 200 miles (321 kilometers) looking for birds. He was able to catch eighty different kinds. Altogether, he collected more than five thousand different organisms. Some of them were alive. He even kept one tortoise he had caught as a pet. Nobody is exactly sure what happened to Darwin's pet tortoise. Many people believe that it was eventually given to a zoo in Australia. The tortoise at the zoo lived to be 176 years old. It died in 2006.

Darwin did not look only at living animals. He also collected many fossils. Some of the fossils did not look anything like the animals Darwin saw on his trip. Yet, other fossils were very similar to living animals. One of the fossils Darwin found was of a *glyptodont*. A glyptodont is huge. In fact, it is about the size of a car. It has armor similar to that of an armadillo. Darwin wondered about this. The two animals were obviously different. So, why did they look so similar? And why were glyptodonts no longer living?

Darwin thought that the glyptodont might be an ancestor of the modern-day armadillo. The specimens that Darwin collected made him realize that living things do not vary only from one continent or environment to another. Something also causes them to vary over time. The process by which living things change and develop over time is called **evolution**.

Darwin thought that glyptodonts were related to modern-day armadillos, even though glyptodonts were much larger. They died out about ten thousand years ago.

Darwin did not yet know what caused evolution. Darwin found many birds on the Galápagos Islands. He didn't think these birds were very important. He thought they were different types of blackbirds, wrens, and warblers. Yet, some of the specimens he collected were going to give him a big clue to the cause of evolution.

Darwin saw many similarities between armadillos and glyptodonts. These similarities helped persuade him that living things change over time.

Darwin traveled on the HMS *Beagle* for five years. By the end of his trip, he was homesick. He couldn't wait to see his family. As soon as his ship arrived in England, he rushed home. He got to his hometown late at night, and everybody in his house was asleep. Darwin didn't want to wake anyone up, so he slipped upstairs to his old bedroom. In the morning he shocked everybody by showing up at the breakfast table.

Putting It All Together

Darwin collected many specimens of birds. He sent these specimens to bird experts. They were able to tell what kind of bird each specimen was. When Darwin returned from his voyage on the *Beagle*, the experts had some surprising news for him.

The birds that Darwin took from the Galápagos Islands were not from many different bird families. They were not blackbirds, wrens, and warblers. They were all finches. Yet, they were unlike any other finches found in the world. The news stunned Darwin. How could birds that looked so different from each other be so closely related?

The bird experts had more news for Darwin. It was true that the Galápagos finches were different than all other finches. However, they seemed to be closely related to the finches on the west coast of South America. Since South America was not far from the Galápagos Islands, Darwin realized that the Galápagos finches must have originally come from that continent. Over time, though, the finches on each island began to change. They were evolving.

Darwin learned that all of the finches on the Galápagos Islands were related to the finches in South America. He theorized that the Galápagos finches had changed over time.

Darwin wanted to test his idea. How much could a living thing change over time? He decided to explore this question by breeding pigeons. Pigeons, like other living things, have **variation** in their population. Some pigeons are bigger than others. Some have darker feathers. Some have straighter beaks. Darwin chose a characteristic he wanted to try to change: the size of the neck. He began by mating birds with the thickest necks he could find. Their chicks also had thick necks. Then Darwin mated these chicks with other pigeons that had thick necks. After several generations, he developed a group of pigeons that looked very different from the birds he started with.

Darwin did not study only living pigeons. He also collected dead ones. He found as many different types of pigeons as he could. He kept their skeletons and compared them with each other. He was very interested in how the bones were different from each other. He noticed that some pigeons had slightly longer bones. Other pigeons had bones that were thicker. Different kinds of pigeons also had bones that were slightly different shapes. Darwin thought these differences were very important. They showed that organisms could change.

Darwin bred many different pigeons. He changed how the pigeons looked by mating only those that had certain features.

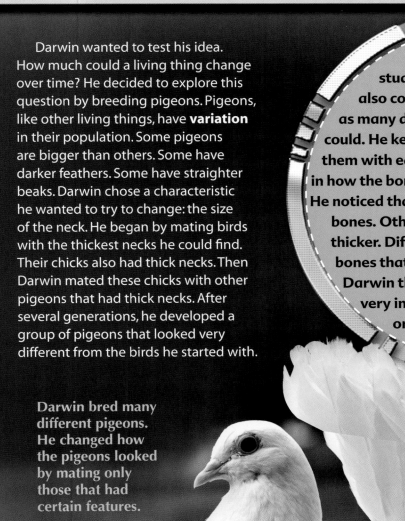

Evolution by Natural Selection

Darwin thought that the kinds of changes that resulted from breeding pigeons also occurred naturally. An animal's environment could cause it to change. Yet, this change did not happen in one generation. Instead, it took thousands of generations.

Darwin knew that individual organisms did not change. Instead, populations changed. Not all of the offspring born to a population can survive. Some of the offspring will die. Only some will grow into adults. Also, only some of these adults will have offspring. And, again, only some of these offspring will survive. This made Darwin think. What determined which offspring would survive?

Not all of the individuals in a population will survive and have offspring.

This moth's coloring helps it blend into its environment. This makes it hard for predators to find the moth. The moth's coloring is an adaptation.

Darwin also knew that there is variation within populations. For example, think about cats. Some cats have stripes. Others are solid colors. Some cats are very small, while others are quite large. These variations are important. In fact, a certain variation could help a cat survive in a particular environment. Imagine a group of cats living in a dense forest. The cats with dark-colored fur are harder to see in the dim woods, so it is easier for them to sneak up on their prey. They are more successful hunters than the light-colored cats and therefore have a higher survival rate.

Suppose, though, that the cats lived in a snowy area. Birds could easily see the black cats approaching. The birds would escape before those cats could pounce.

When a characteristic of a population changes to match the environment, the change is called an *adaptation*. Adaptations can be body parts, such as fur and claws. An adaptation can also be a behavior.

There are many kinds of adaptations. One kind of adaptation is called mimicry. In mimicry, one type of organism looks like another type of organism. For example, a scarlet king snake looks very similar to a coral snake. Both snakes have black, red, and yellow stripes. Both snakes are about the same size. The coral snake is very dangerous. It has deadly poison in its fangs. Because of this, predators avoid the coral snake. The scarlet king snake, on the other hand, is harmless. It has no poison. Yet, predators avoid the scarlet king snake because it looks so much like the coral snake.

Animals that are well adapted to their environment have a better chance of surviving. Animals that are not adapted to their environment are less likely to survive. An animal that reproduces passes its **traits** on to its offspring. This is called heredity. Offspring look like their parents because of heredity.

Offspring inherit many of parents' adaptations. Therefore, they are more likely to survive and have offspring of their own. These offspring, in turn, are also more likely to survive and have their own offspring. In this way, variations are passed on to the next generation and helpful traits spread throughout a population. Darwin called this process **natural selection**.

Natural selection causes a population to change. Remember that not every individual in a population can survive. Many individuals die before they have offspring. Only the best-adapted individuals are likely to survive, reproduce, and have descendents. Descendents include an individual's offspring, their offspring, and so on.

All organisms that exist today are descended from ancient organisms. Yet, not all organisms have exactly the same ancestors. Over time, organisms move from one place to another, or their environment changes around them. Organisms adapt to these changes and continue to have offspring that reflect those adaptations.

Darwin realized this, and he thought that related organisms must have evolved from common ancestors. For example, his finches probably came from the same ancestor in South America. Similarly, tigers, lions, and cheetahs probably had the same ancient cat ancestor. The same was true for other closely related animals.

Natural selection is not the only way that populations evolve. Other things can also cause a population to change. For example, female peacocks are called peahens. Peahens choose their mates by looking at their mates' tails. Peahens are attracted to certain colors and patterns. If a peacock has the right colors and patterns on his tail, he will attract a mate who will then be able to have offspring. So, the peahen has an important role. She helps select which traits will be passed on to the next generation of peacocks.

Natural Selection at Work

1

Organisms produce more offspring than can survive. This increases the chance that at least one will survive. There is variation among organisms in a population. This population of lizards varies in skin color.

2

The organisms that are best adapted to an environment are more likely to survive. In this case, the yellow lizards are hard for the hawk to see, so more yellow lizards survive. They have offspring.

3

Yellow lizards become more common in the population.

Going Public

Darwin was a very careful scientist. He did not want to write about his ideas of natural selection until he was sure they were right. He spent many years collecting evidence, but he still wasn't ready to go public. A young man named Alfred Russel Wallace changed Darwin's mind.

As it turned out, Wallace had come up with ideas that were very similar to Darwin's. This made Darwin realize he shouldn't wait any longer to share his observations with the public. A few months later, Darwin published his book. It was called *The Origin of Species by Means of Natural Selection*. It sold out on the first day.

Darwin became an overnight sensation. Everybody was talking about his book. Scientists began taking sides. It was only a matter of time before the sides clashed. Sure enough, a few months after the book came out, there was a formal debate.

Darwin's ideas were attacked by Samuel Wilberforce. Wilberforce was an effective public speaker, but he was not a scientist. Many of his friends were, however, and they prepared him for the debate.

Samuel Wilberforce argued against Darwin's ideas.

Thomas Huxley debated Wilberforce in support of Darwin's ideas. Huxley was a well-respected scientist. He was also known for his combative nature. Huxley knew that Darwin was worried about what people would think of his book. He told Darwin to relax. Huxley wrote about the debate, "I am sharpening up my claws and beak in readiness."

Huxley was true to his word. He and Wilberforce faced off in front of a large audience. The debate was fierce, but Huxley won. He convinced most of the people in attendance that Darwin was right.

Darwin was very humble. He was also a quiet man. Public speaking made him nervous, so he never joined any of the debates about evolution. Instead, he allowed Thomas Huxley to speak for him. Darwin had told Huxley about his ideas many years before. Huxley had not agreed with them. Over the years, though, Darwin continued to collect evidence. He would present the new evidence to Huxley. Huxley eventually changed his mind. He became Darwin's primary supporter.

Thomas Huxley defended Darwin's ideas. He called himself "Darwin's bulldog."

Questions Darwin Still Had:

Where does variation come from?

Can organisms develop new traits?

How does heredity work?

How old is Earth?

How fast does evolution happen?

Does evolution happen at a steady pace?

Queen Victoria was going to honor Darwin. She was planning to give him a knighthood for his work in science. Then his book came out. Many of her advisors found the book upsetting. They convinced her to give the knighthood to somebody else. Years later, Queen Victoria changed her mind. She decided to honor Darwin upon his death. She allowed him to be buried at Westminster Cathedral near Isaac Newton. Only the most respected British citizens are allowed to be buried there.

At the close of the debate, Joseph Dalton Hooker stood up. Hooker was a famous scientist and an expert in biology. He said that he had long been against the idea that living things evolved. However, Darwin's research changed his mind. Hooker said, "Facts in this science which before were inexplicable to me became, one by one, explained by this theory." He then said he was sure Darwin's ideas were correct.

The debate did not convince everybody, though. Darwin knew why. There were still many holes in his theory. First of all, Darwin did not know what caused variation between individuals. Where did this variation come from? Darwin also did not know how traits were inherited. It was obvious that children looked like their parents, but children were not identical to their parents. There were differences. Darwin had no idea how to explain this.

The final problem with Darwin's theory seemed like a big one: proving the age of the Earth. Earth was inhabited by thousands of different kinds of living things. Darwin knew it would take a very long time for all of these living things to evolve. So, he was sure that Charles Lyell was right about how old Earth was.

In fact, Earth was probably billions of years old. However, the most famous scientist in the United Kingdom, Lord Kelvin, disagreed with this estimate. Lord Kelvin thought Earth had once been a ball of molten rock. Over time, it slowly cooled down. Kelvin used this idea to calculate Earth's age. According to Kelvin, Earth was only about 100 million years old. This was a big problem for Darwin's theory. One hundred million years was not enough time for all the living things on Earth to evolve.

Lord Kelvin thought Earth was a piece of the Sun that had broken off and formed a planet. Over time, the piece cooled down. Kelvin used the difference between Earth's and the Sun's temperatures to calculate Earth's age.

The Evidence Builds

When Darwin died, many of his questions remained unanswered. It did not take long, though, for more evidence to be found. A few years after Darwin died, Lord Kelvin was proven wrong.

As it turned out, Earth was much older than 100 million years. Scientists discovered that Earth is not cooling, as Kelvin thought. So, because Earth was not cooling, Kelvin's calculations were wrong. In fact, scientists were later able to date several rocks on Earth and prove that Earth was about 4 billion years old. Lyell and Darwin were right about Earth's age, which meant there had been plenty of time for all the living things on Earth to evolve.

Earth's age is confirmed by fossils. The oldest fossils ever found are of bacteria. They are about 3.4 billion years old. These fossils were not found until about one hundred years after Darwin's death. When Darwin was alive, there were huge gaps in the fossil record. Darwin knew these gaps were a problem. He wrote, "of this history we possess the last volume alone." He meant that there was not enough information to know all the things that had happened to different organisms over hundreds of millions of years.

This fossil record shows how life on Earth has changed over time.

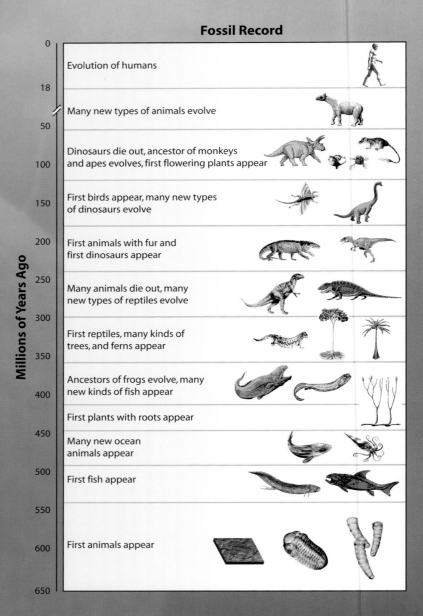

Fossil Record

Millions of Years Ago

0	Evolution of humans
18	
	Many new types of animals evolve
50	
100	Dinosaurs die out, ancestor of monkeys and apes evolves, first flowering plants appear
150	First birds appear, many new types of dinosaurs evolve
200	First animals with fur and first dinosaurs appear
250	Many animals die out, many new types of reptiles evolve
300	First reptiles, many kinds of trees, and ferns appear
350	
400	Ancestors of frogs evolve, many new kinds of fish appear
	First plants with roots appear
450	Many new ocean animals appear
500	First fish appear
550	
600	First animals appear
650	

Luckily, our knowledge has increased since Darwin's time. Many new fossils have been found. The gaps are being filled. In fact, recent finds have helped fill in over 250 gaps in the fossil record. For example, since Darwin's death scientists have found many fossils of whale ancestors. The fossils show how whales evolved over time.

For many years, scientists were not sure what whales evolved from. Then, in 1978, paleontologist Phil Gingerich made an important discovery. He pulled a 52 million-year-old skull out of the ground in Pakistan. The skull fascinated him. It was similar to a wolf-like animal that had lived around 60 million years ago. Yet, there were differences. The ear bones weren't like those of other land animals. They were like those of whales. Gingerich realized what he had found: the skull of the earliest-known whale ancestor.

The oldest fossils ever found are similar to these structures. They are fossilized bacteria. The fossils are around 3.4 billion years old.

Whales came from land animals called *mesonychids*. These land animals slowly changed over time. Originally, they were able to swim in water and walk on land. However, the descendents of these animals had shorter legs. This means they probably spent most of their time in the water. Other fossils continued to show changes in the legs. Eventually, they were shaped more like fins and looked similar to those found in modern whales.

Modern whales still have hip bones. The hip bones have no function. They are only **vestigial structures** from when their ancestors walked on land. The wings on a flightless bird are another example of a vestigial structure. Vestigial structures give clues to an animal's ancestry. A vestigial structure has no function in the organism. It is just a trace of an organ that was once useful to the organism's ancestor.

This fossil record shows that whales and dolphins evolved from animals that lived on land.

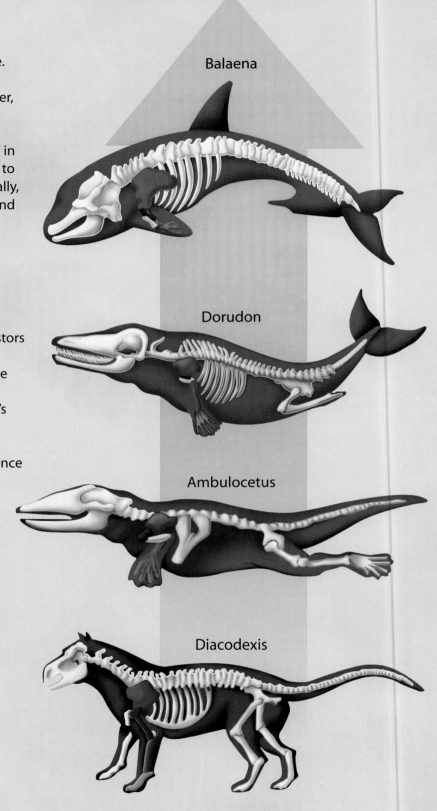

Balaena

Dorudon

Ambulocetus

Diacodexis

More evidence for evolution comes from **homologous structures**. These structures, which are shared by related groups of animals, were inherited from a common ancestor. Bird wings are one example of a homologous structure. There are many different kinds of birds, and they all have wings. This shows that the first bird ancestor had wings. Bird wings have the same bones as lizard legs, so birds and lizards share a homologous structure. This shows that birds and lizards are related.

Homologous structures can be seen in embryos, which are developing babies. Scientists have studied the embryos of many different animals. They were surprised that some embryos were very similar, such as embryos of a cat and a snake.

Look at the similarities between the bones in a human arm, a dog leg, and a seal flipper. Though there are many differences, there are also many similarities.

Not all structures that are similar to each other are homologous. There are also **analogous structures.** They are similar, but they do not come from a common ancestor. Instead, they evolved separately. An example of analogous structures are bird wings and bat wings. Birds evolved from lizardlike animals. Bats evolved from batlike animals. The wings of birds and bats are only similar because they have similar functions. They are both used for flying.

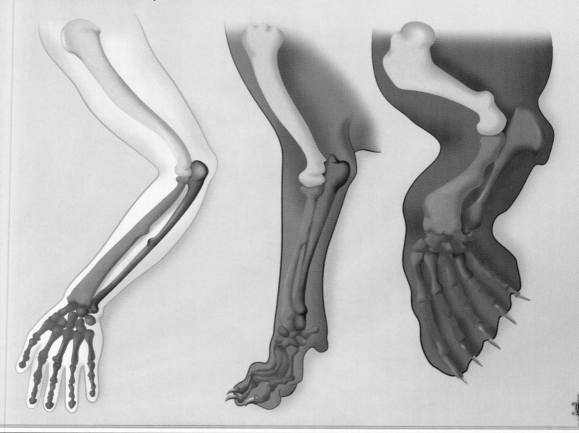

Snakes, chickens, opossums, cats, and bats look very different. Yet, their embryos are surprisingly alike. They are almost the same shape. They have similar structures. They also develop in a similar way, following a common pattern. This suggests that all of these animals have a common ancestor.

Other evidence also supports the idea that different organisms come from the same ancestor, but changed over time. Remember Darwin's finches? Like the finches, other closely related organisms—for example, chimpanzees and orangutans—have many similarities, but also display important differences. These differences are caused by natural selection. The organisms adapt to better fit their environment.

Snake
Natrix natrix

Chicken
Gallus gallus

Possum
Trichosurus vulpecula

Cat
Felis catus

Bat
Rhynchonycteris naso

The development of related organisms is very similar.

Patterns can also be seen in organisms that are not closely related. There are many similar environments around the world. Forests, deserts, and grasslands can be found on all the continents. Animals that live on different continents are usually not closely related to each other. Yet, they may look very similar if they live in similar environments. The animals have all evolved similar adaptations that make them suited to their environments.

Remember that adaptations come from variations within a population. Darwin did not know what caused these variations. He also didn't know how important the answer to this question was. The answer would open a whole new field of science called genetics. It would also provide the biggest piece of evidence for the theory of evolution.

One of the first people to notice the similarities in embryos was German scientist Ernst Haeckel. He lived at the same time as Darwin. Haeckel thought Darwin was correct. He was so sure the theory of evolution was right that he made up organisms that he thought must have existed in the past. He gave the fictional organisms names. He even described what they should look like. He then sent his students on digs to find fossils of these organisms. Amazingly, some of his students were successful. They found fossils that were similar to Haeckel's imaginary organisms.

Kangaroos and jack rabbits are very distantly related. The share similar physical traits. This is because they live in similar environments and have similar adaptations.

Genetics
The Nuts and Bolts of Evolution

Where does variation come from? How does heredity work? These questions stumped Darwin, and he never learned the answers. During Darwin's lifetime, however, another man began putting together the pieces of the puzzle.

Gregor Mendel was a monk. He lived at a monastery in Austria. Mendel was very interested in heredity. He wanted to understand how traits were passed from parents to their offspring.

Mendel had cultivated plants before and had seen a strange pattern. Sometimes a trait such as flower color would show up in the offspring. For example, the seeds from a plant with blue flowers would usually grow other plants with blue flowers. However, sometimes this didn't happen. The seeds from a plant with blue flowers might grow plants with pink flowers. But the seeds from these pink-flowered offspring might grow a blue-flowered plant. What was going on?

Gregor Mendel was an Austrian monk. He carried out his research at a monastery. He eventually became the abbot, or leader, of the monastery.

Mendel cross-pollinated pea plants. He first cut off the stamens on the purple flowers. Stamens make pollen. He then took pollen from the white flowers. He used this to pollinate the purple flowers. The purple flowers grew seeds. The seeds grew into purple-flowered plants.

Mendel decided to investigate this mystery by cross-pollinating pea plants. Pollen is the powdery substance that fertilizes the plant. **Pollination** is what has to happen for a plant to produce a seed. Cross-pollination means the pollen of one plant is used to fertilize another.

Mendel studied flower color, seed color, and plant height. However, he studied only one of these traits at a time. Mendel began with plants that only produced other plants with the same trait. For example, he used a purple-flowered pea plant that only had offspring with purple flowers when the plant pollinated itself. Then he chose a white-flowered pea plant that only had offspring with white flowers when the plant pollinated itself. Mendel took pollen from the white-flowered plant and used it to pollinate the purple-flowered plant.

The plant made seeds. The seeds all grew into plants with purple flowers. Mendel was surprised. Why were there no plants with white flowers? He decided to do another experiment.

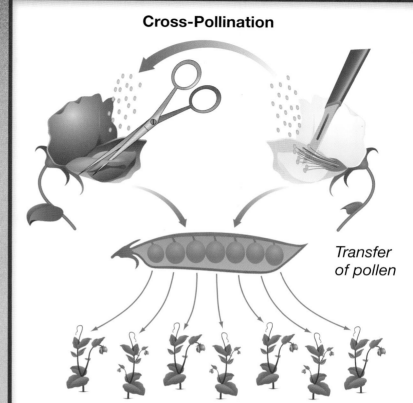

Cross-Pollination

Transfer of pollen

Today, Mendel's pea plant experiment is famous. Yet, it took a long time for other scientists to notice it. Mendel first wrote a paper about his work in 1866. Few people read it. The few who did read it did not understand its importance. This saddened Mendel. He eventually gave up on his experiments. Mendel died in 1883. Seventeen years later a young German scientist found Mendel's paper by chance. The scientist realized how important it was. He republished Mendel's results along with his own research on the subject.

Mendel let the offspring self-pollinate. They grew seeds and Mendel planted them. Then a strange thing happened. Most of the seeds grew into plants with purple flowers, but a few of the seeds grew into plants with white flowers. The trait for white flowers had come back!

Mendel repeated this experiment many times. He always got the same results in the second generation of plants. For every three plants with purple flowers, there was one plant with white flowers. Mendel realized that each plant must have two sets of instructions for a trait. Each parent donated a set. One set was dominant over the other. For example, the instructions for purple flowers were dominant. If a plant had instructions for both purple and white flowers, it would only grow purple flowers. It would have to have two sets of instructions for white flowers in order to grow white flowers.

The sets of instructions Mendel discovered are now called *genes*. Mendel did not know what genes were made of. In fact, it took another one hundred years for scientists to find out where these instructions were in cells. They learned that genes are found in **DNA**. All cells have DNA. The genes in DNA control how the cell grows. Genes also control all of the cell's activities.

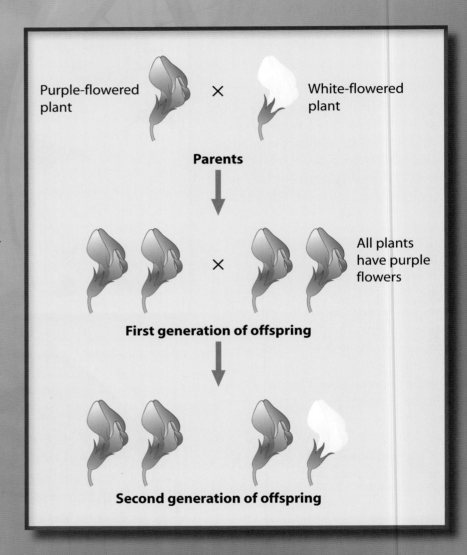

Purple-flowered plant × White-flowered plant

Parents

All plants have purple flowers

First generation of offspring

Second generation of offspring

Mendel found that heredity occurs in patterns. On average, the second generation would have one white-flowered plant for every three purple-flowered plants.

Genes determine what traits a living thing has. Whenever a cell divides, it makes a copy of its genes for the new cell. Sometimes, though, the genes are not copied perfectly. The differences can result in new variations. These variations are then passed on to following generations.

In 1944 the American scientist Oswald Avery discovered that genes were found in DNA. Until this time, scientists did not know the purpose of DNA inside cells.

All living things on Earth have DNA. DNA is made up of four different kinds of chemicals. These four chemicals are adenine (A), thymine (T), guanine (G), and cytosine (C). The order of these chemicals in DNA makes up a code. The code tells the cell how to make certain proteins. All the structures in your body are made out of proteins. The code CCT is for a protein called proline. This is one of the proteins used by your body to make blood. All humans have the code CCT in their DNA.

It's in the Genes

The discovery of genes changed how scientists viewed evolution. Scientists came to understand that natural selection does not work only on populations and organisms. Natural selection also works on genes.

Every organism has two sets of the same genes. When organisms reproduce, each parent passes on a set of genes so that the offspring will have one set from each parent. So, the offspring's genes are similar to those of each parent, but not identical. This is one way that variation occurs.

Variation also comes from changes in genes. Most of the time when a gene changes it does not affect the organism. Sometimes a change in a gene can have a harmful effect. The organism may not survive. Yet, a few gene changes are useful. They cause the organism to have a new adaptation. If the adaptation is very helpful, the organism will be more likely to survive. It will pass on the useful gene to many of its offspring.

Scientists have learned that some genes don't seem to be very important. You can change these genes without changing the organism. A few genes, though, are critical.

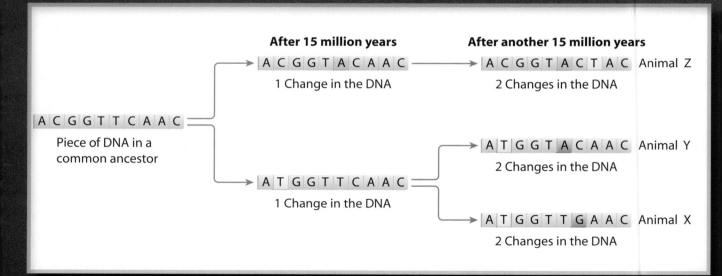

After 15 million years

A C G G T A C A A C
1 Change in the DNA

After another 15 million years

A C G G T A C T A C Animal Z
2 Changes in the DNA

A C G G T T C A A C
Piece of DNA in a common ancestor

A T G G T A C A A C Animal Y
2 Changes in the DNA

A T G G T T C A A C
1 Change in the DNA

A T G G T T G A A C Animal X
2 Changes in the DNA

Genes change at a relatively steady rate. The changes cause new types of organisms to evolve. Scientists can count the number of differences in the DNA of different organisms. This tells scientists how closely related the organisms are.

These critical genes, called Hox genes, control the shape and size of body parts. Hox genes also decide how an embryo grows. They determine where the arms and legs should be. They control where the eyes grow in the head. They also cause the organs to form in the right place.

A small change to a Hox gene can drastically change how an organism looks. Scientists have studied Hox genes in insects. By moving a single Hox gene, they caused a fruit fly to grow legs out of its head. If you remove the same gene, the fruit fly grows one less pair of legs than it should. An alteration in a single Hox gene can also cause an entire new group of organisms to evolve!

A genome is a complete set of genes for a type of organism. Humans are all the same type of organism, so all humans have the same genome. Recently, scientists mapped the human genome. Humans have enough DNA to have about one billion genes. However when scientists mapped the genome, they found that most of the DNA in humans is something called junk DNA. It has no use. In fact, human DNA only contains about 25,000 genes. This small number of genes controls the growth and development of every cell, tissue, and organ in the human body.

Scientists changed a Hox gene in this fruit fly. The change caused legs to grow out of the fly's head.

Putting Natural Selection to the Test

Evolution happens over millions of years. This makes it difficult to observe. Yet, small evolutionary changes can be seen. Scientists have observed small changes both in labs and in nature. Scientists have even seen natural selection at work.

Peter and Rosemary Grant are professors at Princeton University. They studied birds in the wild. The evidence they collected showed natural selection at work.

Remember Darwin's finches? When Darwin first saw them, he didn't think they were all in the same family of birds. Instead, he thought they were blackbirds, wrens, and warblers. When Darwin learned they were all finches, he **hypothesized** that they had a common ancestor. He thought their different beak shapes evolved because of their different diets. This seemed like a reasonable idea, but most scientists thought the idea could not be tested. Peter and Rosemary Grant disagreed. They moved to the Galápagos Islands to put natural selection to the test.

The Grants did their research on Daphne Major. It is one of the Galápagos Islands.

The United Nations made the Galápagos Islands a World Heritage site in 1978. The islands were given this designation because they are a living museum and a showcase of evolution. The islands only make up about 3,042 square miles (7,880 square kilometers) of land. That's not much bigger than the state of Rhode Island. Yet, the islands are home to more than one thousand kinds of plants and animals that are found nowhere else on Earth. Many of these plants and animals are threatened by extinction. Because of this, in 2007, the United Nations placed the Galápagos Islands on a list of World Heritage sites in danger.

If Darwin was right, two things must be true. First, the finch population must have a large variety of genes for different beak shapes so that beak shape can evolve. Second, certain beak shapes must improve an organism's ability to survive.

The Grants decided to do their experiment on the island of Daphne Major. They started by capturing and tagging almost all the finches on the island. They then began tracking the finches. They recorded which finches died and which survived. They also recorded which finches had babies. In addition, they measured the size of the finches and also the shape of their beaks. The Grants continued their research for over thirty years.

The Grants constantly analyzed their data. Eventually they saw that Darwin's first assumption was true. There was a large amount of variation in the finch population. Birds from the same original group developed a wide range of beak sizes.

Next, the Grants saw that beak size affected survival rates. Some years there were droughts. Food became scarce. During these years, birds with larger beaks had a better chance of surviving. This is because the birds with large beaks were able to feed on the larger, tougher seeds. The birds with smaller beaks were not able to eat these seeds.

After a drought, the average beak size of the entire finch population increased dramatically. This surprised the Grants. They didn't expect natural selection to act so quickly. Yet, a change in the food supply had caused the finches to evolve within a few decades. Those with small beaks had a greater death rate and therefore did not reproduce.

The Grants realized something else from their research. Variation in a population was extremely important. If the finch population didn't have a variety of beak sizes, they would not have been able to survive the drought. None of the finches would have been able to eat the larger, tougher seeds. All the finches on Daphne Major would have died out. However, those with larger beaks were able to adapt to the change in the environment. So, the more variation a population has, the more likely it is to evolve and survive.

The Grants studied the medium ground finch for more than twenty years.

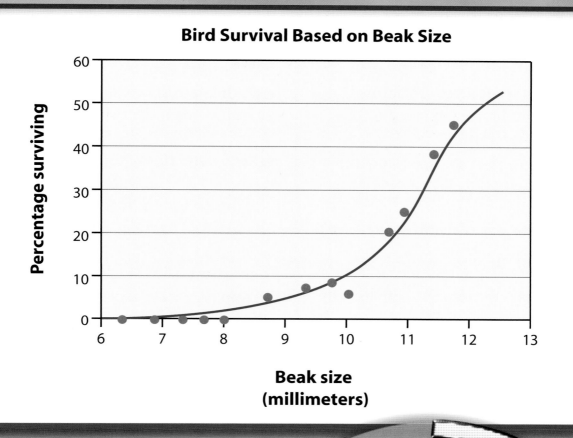

Bird Survival Based on Beak Size

During periods of drought, finches with larger beaks had a better chance of surviving. This caused the average beak size of the finch population to increase.

Many other experiments have confirmed Darwin's ideas. Today, the theory of evolution is the foundation of biology. It helps explain observations made in all branches of life science. Scientists are still debating parts of the theory. For example, nobody is certain exactly how each different kind of animal arose. Scientists no longer question whether evolution takes place. Scientists have realized that understanding evolution is the key to understanding the natural world.

All of the finches on the Galápagos Islands are closely related. Yet, there are different species, or groups, of finches on the island. When members of the same species mate, their offspring are also able to mate and have their own offspring. If two kinds of finches are no longer able to mate and have fertile offspring, this means they are no longer the same species. To understand this idea, think about donkeys and horses. Donkeys and horses are closely related. They can mate. Their offspring are mules. Yet, mules can't have offspring. They are infertile. This means that donkeys and horses are different species.

Glossary

analogous structures Structures that look similar to one another but evolved separately.

adapt Adjust oneself to a new situation.

biology Science of living things.

DNA Deoxyribonucleic acid; hereditary material that controls the activities of a cell.

environment The place where an organism lives.

evolution The gradual development of a species over time.

generation Offspring having a common parent; a single step in the line of descent.

homologous structures Structures that are shared by related groups of animals.

hypothesize Create an explanation on uncertain grounds.

natural selection Process by which organisms with adaptations survive and pass the adaptations to their offspring.

pollination The transfer of pollen to the female part of a plant, causing seed production.

theory In science, a unifying explanation for a broad range of hypotheses and observations.

trait A characteristic that an organism has.

variation Slight differences in characteristics.

vestigial structure The remnant of a once-useful body part.

Find Out More

Books

Gamlin, Linda. *Eyewitness: Evolution.* New York: DK Children, 2001.
Strong visuals support clear explanation of the theory of evolution.

Jenkins, Steve. *Life on Earth: The Story of Evolution.* Boston: Houghton Mifflin, 2002.
Includes beautiful illustrations to accompany the story of evolution from
the beginning of life on Earth through millions of years of its history.

Lawson, Kristan. *Darwin and Evolution for Kids: His Life and Ideas with 21 Activities.*
Chicago: Chicago Review Press, 2003.
Describes the life and studies of Charles Darwin. Includes activities that illustrate
his studies and findings.

Websites

http://explore-evolution.unl.edu/
The University of Nebraska State Museum offers an evolution website.

http:// www.howstuffworks.com/search.php?terms=evolution
This website offers multiple articles explaining how evolution works, how it relates
to dinosaurs, and what evolution means to humans.

http:// www.pbs.org/wgbh/evolution/
The PBS website discusses many aspects of evolution, including its past,
the history of the science, and how it relates to religion.

Index